5 Proven Principles To Becoming A More Confident Woman

Alesia Dowden

"The Confidence Coach"

Heels Too High

ISBN 978-1-0913-1068-1 (pbk)

Printed in United States America

This book is dedicated to

My daughters, Nela, Nina and Mercedes, and to my granddaughters Neriah, Milania, Aayilah, Lillian and Olivia. My desire is that you each will always first and foremost call upon the name of Jesus Christ our Lord & Savior for direction and love, and to consider yourself only as He sees you – one which has been created in His image. That you never find a reason to compare yourself to anyone but always be reminded that the Lord God made you on purpose, with purpose, and to fulfill a purpose.

You are loved!

CONTENTS

Matthew 5:14 - 16

14: "You are the light of the world. A town built on a hill cannot be hidden.

15: Neither do people light a lamp and put it under a bowl. Instead they put it on its stand, and it gives light to everyone in the house.

*16: In the same way, **let your light shine before others, that they may see your good deeds and glorify your Father in heaven**.*

NIV Bible

Acknowledgements

Thank you to:

Randy Dowden my husband of whom I love and respect. Thank you, my Love, for always letting me be me yet directing me through your actions and disciplined life. I love you man!

To my daughters Nela & Nina, who inspire me daily simply by being who they are! I love and adore you both so much, you are awesome daughters, I am proud to say you are mine!

Leola Jones my eldest sister for always being my cheerleader and the example of a God-fearing woman, as well as my best friend. For your prayers and endeavors to keep me focused on the vision God purposed me to live out.

Pastors Michael and Dorelle Arnwine, and Asst. Pastor Jerry & Minister Brenda Holmes who are more than my spiritual leaders and advisors, but you are also my friends.

Alesia Dowden

Introduction

Designed with purpose, to fulfill a purpose, on purpose, yes that is you. In you rest the gift of purpose which can only be birthed by you, a gift that when cultivated will cause change to come not only in your life but those who surround you.

Have you ever asked yourself, "What am I designed to accomplish"? In order to live a fulfilled life at some point you will be required to address this question. Finding the answer is not always easy, you may have to search diligently for her much like I did. But when you find her, "Purpose"... she is a treasure much worth finding. Underneath the wings of purpose peace is found, in that place love and joy also flourish. It is underneath the wings of purpose that you will be able to live the golden rule, "do unto others as you would have them do unto you". Jealousy, envy and strife are removed, because when purpose shows up she reminds you of how unique you are and that God crafted you with His hands and what a glorious being you are – only one of you exist – wow – You Can Stand Confident.

As you begin your journey to discovering your purpose and becoming a more confident you, begin by asking yourself, "What do I want?" You see it is only when you discover what you really want, and you are willing to count up the cost of what it will take to achieve your purpose will the strength come to move you to act upon your vision. "Knowing", is the beginning of cracking the confidence code. It is only then that you will begin to walk with confidence and will be prepared to overcome all obstacles that present themselves.

Knowing what you want will cause you to look for opportunities and be open when they reveal themselves to you. You will no longer walk around with blinders on, but you will begin to seek out opportunities that are in line with your purpose. Each opportunity that comes your way will require you to make a decision. The harvest which is produced when making the right decision based on the opportunity presented will cause confidence to become a part of your very nature and character. Right decisions come from surrounding yourself with people who walk in wisdom.

Making the wrong decision can be detrimental to your growth as you begin to walk with confidence in your purpose. Why, you might ask. Wrong decisions often produce fear – fear stifles and is a confidence killer. Think about the last time you made a decision that bore a disastrous outcome; oh boy, I've had a few of those stories. If you are like most people, it took you a while before you set out on another opportunity which could yield a benefit.

Some decisions in life will require you to reach out to people which have your best interest at hand. I call these people your "Core of Influence". Those in your core of influence hold you in high regards, in other words they see and understand your purpose and are willing to push you towards greatness. They are not offended by your increase. They simply want what's best for you and won't hesitate to tell you when they believe you are moving in the wrong direction. This group consists of only a few people, approximately 3 to 6 at most, which have already begun to walk in their purpose thereby being excellent examples and stewards that will lead you with confidence.

The core of influence is so great at producing confidence because they have learned to reach beyond their immediate surroundings and push pass limitations. They have discovered that knowledge is not only power, but that applied knowledge is powerful, therefore they seek out those who have applied knowledge; mentors which have been there, done that and accomplished it quite well. Some call it networking, but I call it relationship building. It is easy to walk into your purpose with confidence when you have people mentoring you that have already walked along a road much like yours. In all your getting, get wisdom. But note... the beginning is knowledge is the fearing of God.

Purpose begins and ends with FAITH. Without faith it is impossible to please God. Without faith, confidence does not exist.

Confidence = Knowing + Decision + Direction + Mentorship + Faith

Please read on...

Alesia Dowden

1

And Her Heels Went Klick

ALESIA: My Heels Are Not Too High, This Is My Walk
(Isaiah 49:1)

As I kicked one leg out from under the cover, then threw back the sheet and comforter from the rest of my body, I reluctantly got out of bed. With an early morning haze lingering, eyes barely opened I drugged myself around the corner of the bedroom into the washroom. There before me in the mirror stood a woman half-awake with hair everywhere. She stared back at me and I could hear the words rambling through her brain, "Do I really want to do this", "I hope they are not just going to try to sell me something else that's not going to add value to my life". Yes, that was me. After standing there looking in the mirror for a few minutes more trying to convince myself why I didn't need to go to the conference, my body slowly turned toward the shower and my hand reached down to turned on the faucet.

Thirty minutes later I was almost completely dressed and ready for the day, just needed to put on my glass slippers. I walked over to the closet and slide the door back, there were my girls, my glass slippers, my high heels. Because I didn't want to over pack, I only grabbed two pair of heels to take with me on this trip. While packing I remember thinking to myself, "take two pair of shoes that could be worn with all three of the dresses in my suitcase", so I grabbed my four-inch black and white leather Sam Edelman's and the four-inch black mess and leather Guess high heels.

My dress for the day was multicolor and had many shades of blue and a pattern which somewhat matched my Sam Edelman's. I reached down grabbed my girls and began to strap them on. Ah, the voice in my head resonated "fabulous", as I looked in the mirror – complete and ready to go now. I kissed my husband goodbye who by the way was still lying in the hotel bed all comfy and cozy, I could see that he too was pleased with the outfit I had selected for the day. Reaching for the doorknob to make my exit into the hallway, with a whisper I said to my husband "Goodbye my love I will see you this evening".

The hotel in which the conference was being held was one of the largest of the Marriott hotel properties in Orlando, Florida. When my husband and I were in the hotel lobby checking in I remembered looking around and thinking to myself, "I could easily get lost in here". The walk from my room to the elevator seemed to take forever and yes, I actually got lost for just a minute or two, I walked around in circles several times - lol. Now, finally standing in front of the elevator waiting for the doors to open I thought to myself "Did I pick the right heels"?

From the twelfth floor to the first floor was a quick ride down in the elevator. As the doors opened, I felt a sense of excitement rising, an adrenaline rush and I kicked into high gear, all senses on go. I began to walk the corridor of the event hall greeting every one of whom I made eye contact; "Good morning and how are you today". A young lady came up quickly behind me and was now right beside me, our strides locked, and our conversation began. I discovered that it was her first time attending the event as well, and she was extremely excited to be here. We shared a few more tidbits about one another before we were interrupted by one of the event greeters. "Welcome to CST, we hope you have the experience of a lifetime". The young hostess stood about 4'7 and was spunky and full of energy. She continued with, "Wow you look fabulous, love the dress and look at those shoes. But how long are you going to wear those shoes, that heel is very high. I bet you'll be in flat tomorrow". I looked down at my feet and thought "My girls are awesome - right" and I responded with, "Nope... the girls have it, once the girls go on, a lady never takes them off", in other words, I would be in high heels all three days of the event. Believe it or not I had this same conversation all throughout the day – "Look at those shoes", and "Don't your feet hurt?"

Wow, I had made it to day three of the event, and yes the day before, on day two I wore another pair of fabulous four inch heels and I received much of the same response, " I don't see how you can walk in those heels, they are way too high for me", yadda, yadda. I was starting to get just a little offended of having to defend my glass slippers every day. I wanted to tell those ladies to mind their own business, to leave my shoes alone, but instead I simply continued to let my feet do the walking.

As day three of the conference was coming to a close, several of the event attendees and I had danced our way to our respective tables, taken pictures with one another and the event speaker, as well as given standing ovations to the host of the event. It had been a spectacular convention. A woman that sat at my table said to me, "Let's go outside to the lobby take some picture in front of the backdrop provided by the organization" and so I followed. As we began to walk through the room she looked down at my feet and then up at me and replied, "You must wear heels all the time, because you've rocked those high heels all week long – you go girl". A big grinned came across my face and I thought, "Finally, someone thought it through and is allowing me to be me. My heels are not too high for me".

As I sat out on the balcony of my hotel suite in the multi-strapped lounge chair with my bare feet propped on the circular glass table reminiscing about the days past and all I had gleaned, my mind drifted back to the many conversations I had about my shoes. "Those heels are cute but they are way too high", "Don't they hurt your feet", "How can you keep those on", I thought to myself, "Don't they know I've been wearing heels since the twelfth grade, what right do they have trying to bully me out of my shoes". I begin to question God as to what the past three days were all about, why the shoe thing... and what was I to learn. I heard a still small voice say to me, "grab your bible, read Matthew chapter one". I immediately picked up my bible and began to read the first chapter of Matthew. The primary focus of this chapter is the genealogy of Christ, yet this time I received a new revelation. Within chapter one, five distinct principles were revealed through the lives of five women named in the genealogy of Christ. As many times as I had read the book of Matthew, I should have seen these principles before. Within the genealogy the mention of five women can be found, I heard the voice tell me to search each of them out and I would find my answer. So, I did. For the next few hours I read each of their stories, but still had questions. As I pondered what I had just read, the stories of these courageous and confident women, my life begin to play back to me and here is what I saw...

Heels Too High – Please read on.

My Mothers Steps

I can remember her walking towards me with a quick pace. As she grew closer, I could hear the noise from her stilettos, "click, click, click" on the sidewalk. It was my Mom coming home from work, she worked as a secretary. You see my Mother didn't drive so daily she would ride the city bus to and from work. My Dad would drive her to the bus-stop in the wee hours of the morning and she would walk home from the bus-stop in the evening. It seems as though she had to walk at least a mile to get to the house, and in heels.

Her fast pace and the sound of her shoes hitting the pavement still ring in my head as an unforgotten memory long after she has been laid to rest. I don't know if that embedded-vision is what has caused me years later to love high heels so much or not, but I believe it does, as often what we see and what appeals to us we mimic. I know you are probably wondering what does that story have to do with me... keep reading.

Easter Shoes

Easter was upon us and Nannie my Father's God-mother had given my parents money to help with our attire, I was around 10 years old. There were five of us at that time, four girls and one boy. Roaming around through Kenny's Shoe store (yes, I'm telling my age) I spotted a pair of white patent leather baby-doll shoes with a clip-on bow, the heel was about one to two inches high. I remember asking my Mom for the shoes, but because she was so busy with my older siblings she simply brushed me aside, I had to wait my turn. I grabbed the shoe off the carousel and took it to my Dad with excitement in my voice, "Daddy, daddy can I have these". He snatched the shoe out of my hand put it back on the carousel, drug me out of the store by the arm, and whispered sternly in my ear as only for me to hear, "those heels are too high for you". With a toss he let go of my arm and turned to walk back in the store and I followed. No crying... in those days crying wasn't allowed, and it didn't get you anywhere at least not with my Dad. I remember being extremely discouraged. My mother having completed her tasks with the other children, chose a pair of white flats for me.

Size 8

Fast forward to high school my senior year. I was coming into my own. I had grown about seven inches taller than I was when I enter high school at 4'11. I'd developed a few curves, not anything to boast about and my Dad had now allowed me to purchase my first pair of heels, "Candies"! They were slip-ons which had a fabricated wooden-like material for the bottom and a wide beige leather strap with four studs holding each side of the strap together, and yes, yes, they were three and a half inches tall. At last my dream had come true; I was floating on air every time I put my Candies on.

I was so I in love with the way I felt when wearing my glass slippers, I decided to wear heels every day to school. The first day, my girlfriends complimented my attire, and so with the second day. About the third day a few others had taken notice. My English class had just ended, and I was headed to the food court area when a class-mate caught up to me. The conversation went something like this, "Those shoes are cute, but... who do you think you are?" The smile on my face was quickly turned upside down as I was being asked to defend my desire to be my confident-self. I didn't say a word, I let my feet do the walking – I will walk like a girl no matter who is watching!

Please read on...

Discovery - - Walk into your purpose

At a very young age I came into the knowledge of Christ and accepted Him as my Lord and Savior. It is the Father which is in heaven that has begun a great work in me, and it is He who will complete that work. Within me He designed a confident trait and I discovered that I didn't need permission to walk in high heels; I just had to put them on and go. People will talk because that is what they do, but the Holy Spirit will lead me, and I will follow – I Will Stand Confident.

As I looked back on my life and its many confident experiences, I discovered that each generation will influence the next. As I watched my mother walking towards me, click, click, click, I saw a woman of confidence full of strength, wisdom, elegance and perseverance with a cause – her family, her purpose. As a toddler I watched my daughters slip on my heels and walk through the house as though they were born to wear them. In their adulthood I see women of confidence, strength, wisdom, elegance, creativeness and character. My grand-daughters, all five of them have gone into granny's closet, selected their favorite pair of high heels and they too clunk down the hallway on the wooden floors with grace. I look forward to the day when they will read this book and be reminded how uniquely designed they are by God.

I discovered that there will be moments in your life that will require you to wait before grasping the prize, but that you are never to give up. I glance back now and hear the voice of reason from my Father's in the shoe store which was simply saying "Not now, you are too young and could hurt yourself, but when you are ready I want you to go for it, I want you to walk tall". Although I didn't quite understand at the time, confidence was building me into the woman I am today.

In high school, classmates that wanted me to comply, to simply be like everyone else ended up causing me to see who I really was. Confidence was building in me, and I refuse to come down for anyone.

Since my first pair of high heels until now, I've discovered that most people will not understand my purpose, nor will they agree with why I do what I do, however, it does not mean that I am required to stop developing, growing or performing to the best of my ability simply because of their lack of understanding. At some point in your life you too will have to let go of the limitations in which others have placed on you and begin to walk with confidence just like I did. Confident, unmoved, unshaken and unashamed to be you! Will it always be easy... the answer is "no", but understand this if you don't start walking with confidence now, if you don't stand confident – when will you?

Back on the balcony, I heard that still small voice say, "teach my daughters to stand confident". It was at that point that the heartbeat of this book began. On the balcony is where God began to reveal to me the distinct principles of how confidence could be gained by anyone willing to apply the five principles of building confidence to their lives. I thought I was attending the conference for one thing, yet God had greater intentions for my life and for you, the reader of this book.

Yes, this is a book about building a more confident you, it's about empowerment but through spiritual growth. As you read through this book you will hear my story and the story of five other remarkable women which overcame bearers in their lives that seemed impossible to overcome.

The five proven principles of becoming a more confident woman will be discussed in the next five chapters. I will need you to go on a journey with me as we peer into each of the lives and households of these women (found in The Book of Matthew chapter one) and ***what might have taken place*** to discover the principles of building confidence there in. Hopefully you will also see yourself and be reminded of the confident traits of which you already possess. My prayer is by the time you finish this book you too will have come to the resolve that you were designed with purpose, on purpose by God Himself, and that nobody can change that. That you will know that you are unstoppable whether in high heels, flats or sneakers that you can and will stand confident.

Read on...

2

Girl... What Do You Want

TAMAR: Take Back What Is Rightfully Yours
(Matthew 6:33)

Principle #1 – Know what you want and be willing to count up the cost to possess it.

I sit in my room, holding two precious miracles from God. Yes, the expectancy was only for one, yet God has chosen to grace me in abundance as He has given me two baby boys, Perez and Zerah.

I have been granted motherhood, that which I have longed for for quite some time now. For you see as a young maiden my father chose a husband for me. I was delighted to become the wife of Er for he was very handsome, strong and masculine and oh yes, let me not forget to tell you he was of the tribe of Judah. I'd heard many conversations and stories from the villagers around about the city how mighty and fierce was the God he and his family served. Did you know their God promised to provide and protect them always? When my father told me that I would be united with such a great family I was elated. I too, could serve a God so mighty and would leave a legacy for generation to come as my children would be blessed, yes truly blessed and covered.

The wedding was amazing, I felt beautiful and radiant, dressed in my wedding garment so colorful and vibrant. I remember dancing around the room as my mother tried pinning my hair. This was my day, my new life, my covering, my blessing.

The ceremony seemed to take forever but I did not care. I was captivated by the moment and of course the handsome man of to whom I was being presented. Glasses filled to the brim with wine which my father had preserved for such a time as this, our fathers and family members toasted and blessed the joining our families and culture. The merriment went on for hours.

As the evening came to a close, I found myself in a state of nervousness and panic; would I be pleasing to my husband, what if I did something wrong, oh my, the "what if's" began to consume my thoughts. I had never lain with a man before. I had to stop myself from becoming so frantic, calm down Tamar, you've got this; stand confident. Your husband will lay with you tonight and you will conceive a child, a man child, your husband will love you all the more, you will be called blessed, and you will be praised at the city gates. Someday your children will praise you speaking well of how you cared for your family.

A few years have gone by now and I am unable to produce a child. My heart is heavy, what was wrong with me; had I angered the God of whom I now serve, the God of Abraham, Isaac and Jacob that He would close my womb. My husband Er, now bitter and cruel as ever was unapproachable and seemed to have become so wicked and nasty that even his closest friends have turned away and want nothing more to do with us. I hardly see him anymore. The days were long, the nights even longer. The silence throughout the house was disconcerting. No cries or laugher from children at play. It was the sound of loneliness, the sound of despair, the sound of an uncomforted heart, a broken heart.

Tears streaming down my face uncontrollably, my heart feeling as though it will stop beating any second now, I'm finding it really hard to breath. Adorned in widow's clothing I sit grieving for my husband, my love, my covering, but he is gone, buried in the field of his father's ancestors. I search my thoughts for understanding, why would God grant me a husband only to take him away so soon – what have I done wrong. Yes, I understand he was wicked, but for some strange reason I still felt love for him and beside I couldn't divorce him, who wants to be called an adulteress for the rest of her life. This was a relationship in which I was damned if I do or don't. What a life, no children and now... no husband. Empty.

After a time of mourning my father-in-law Judah approached me. It was nice to see him, as it had been a while, he was a good man, a family man and there was a joy that resonated within him. For some reason, I always felt like praising or dancing when he was around. He spoke the unexpected. Now I had heard it was a part of their custom, but it was happening to me. Judah offered his second son Onan to be my husband.

Wow, second chances. The God of second chances is who I will praise. For He has given me another husband and another opportunity to bare children. Yes, maybe this time I will give Onan several children, yes, a house full. My new husband and I will be fruitful, and we will multiply. We will be a nation that is called blessed. I will sew garments for my family, prepare meals day and night. I will select the proper field and purchase the land on which we shall build. My heart is over joyed – a second chance.

Again, I adorn widows clothing. My head covered and held low, my womb empty, no life is in me. "Why was this happening to me", I yelled from within. It would have been better for me to have never left my father's house than to be widowed now twice – and twice barren. I am cursed with a curse, that's it. I am convinced as this would never happen to an ordinary woman. This life of mine is full of disappointment. Once again, no love, no children, no covering.

This time I saw pity in his eyes as Judah spoke to me. "Keep on your mourning clothes; go back to your father's house. When my son Shelah is old enough to marry, I will send for you".

I can't believe it, go back to my father's house. I am far too old to still be living in my father's house. What will all my friends say, what will my family say, I'm a walking disgrace. I can hear them now, "The man killer", and "Is she cursed by God or something for she has yet to produce any children yet has had two husbands". They will all laugh and mock me. The strength I once knew is now gone. I am alone now, but confident that in the years to come joy will find me.

Why that scoundrel Judah, how could he. Liar! I am so angry I think I could cry or throw something, maybe both. He stood there looking me straight in the eye and said, "When Shelah is old enough to marry, I will call for you". Liar! All these years, I've sat here ashamed and destitute in my father's house hoping and praying for another chance at life. Waiting for my dreams to be realized. To love again, and how I long to have my belly filled with the movement of my seed. My widow's clothing has worn old and are now faded. My face and body are showing signs of age. Really, I waited...

****

What Are You Waiting On?

Her name is Tamar, far too many years had gone pass and she was still being told to wait for it; does this statement sound familiar. Tamar had setback after setback and had sat back long enough to learn that nothing was going to happen unless she made a conscious decision to go after what she wanted and to conquer all. I can only imagine her fear and frustration as she began to plan out the steps necessary to complete her task and gain her prize.

Tamar's story speaks volume to the women who are listening. The truths and principles we find in her story can be applied to our story today. The bible clearly states in Ecclesiastics 1:9 "there is nothing new under the sun", therefore we are only experiencing an updated version of the joys and sorrows of life along with its issues and concerns wouldn't you agree. Seeds of godly wisdom are sprinkled all throughout her story, and if you look closely you may find a part of your story; I know I did.

As you read between the lines of Tamar's story you will discover that there are a few actions you must take in your pursuit of becoming a more confident woman. 1). She knew what she wanted, and 2). She counted the cost and developed a plan.

Know what you want.

As Tamar's story unfolds, we discover that she is a woman of purpose, passion and persistence. Her desire or goal was to become a mother and she consistently pursued her purpose as she was willing to marry not once, not twice but three times into the same family to achieve her goal. I'm sure women today would contend that after experiencing life with a wicked man why would she want to stick around, hadn't she experienced enough. After all the death of Er released her from the covenant of marriage, she was free to return home to her father's house. But she would have returned home empty handed. Tamar understood her rights under the levirate marriage law, the laws of the time; her rights to heritage, property and covering. She stood firm and went after her dream, with the intent to achieve it; she would not let anything get in her way – she became focused.

So, I pose this question to you, "What do you want?" In my coaching session that is the first question I address with my client. The response is often the same, "I am not sure, let me think about it", therefore they do just that. I allow my client approximately one to two weeks to do some soul searching and then return with a list of things they would like to accomplish.

Confidence begins to reveal itself in our lives when we endeavor to take part in the process of achieving. It doesn't matter what you are trying to achieve, be it building a relationship, building wealth, increasing in spirituality or starting a business, confidence will show up when you start moving forward.

Remember when you first learned how to ride a bike, or the first time you put on a pair of roller skates. I bet you wobbled or even fell down a few times. But eventually you learned and became so confident that you began to teach others. What about that first time you got behind the steering wheel in your Dads car – you were probably scared as all get out, I know I was. But I drive like a pro now. To become successful and confident at any tasks in life, you will first need a made-up mind. Once you put your mind to it, you achieved it, and now you are very confident. Girls, it works every time. And yes, it's as simple as that. "Knowing", in and of itself does not produced confidence but putting action behind the goal does. Once you have discovered what it is that you want, you are able to move forward with purpose.

Be willing to count the cost to get what you want - Plan

Perseverance. After you've answered the question, "What do I want", now life will ask you to make a few sacrifices. There is a quote noted by Napoleon Hill which reads, "Great achievement is usually born out of great sacrifice". Tamar was willing to sacrifice her life. Under the levirate laws, she would have been labelled an adulteress which in turn could have led her to be stoned to death. She was a crafty woman, as she laid out a plan, step by step as to how she would gain her prize. It was deceptive; however, it was a different time and the laws of the land were not as they are today. So, although I don't recommend you operate under the guise of deception to reach your goal, you must put together a plan to achieve your goals. Let your take-away from her story be that Tamar was willing to go above and beyond to get the job done.

I gather the next nine months weren't easy for Tamar. She would now have to live with the consequences of her deception, never again would Judah cleave to her as a wife. In the end Judah admitted that she had every right to have done what she did, yet he wanted nothing more to do with her. Tamar would find satisfaction in the birthing of a child, her vision realized, her dream would come true.

Unbeknownst to Tamar, she would receive a double-portion blessing, two male children would be birthed through her.

How determined are you to gain your prize? Are you willing to think outside the box, the triangle, or the circle that has enclosed or clouded your thinking? During a follow-up coaching session with a young lady I asked her what she wanted. After her soul searching, she said, "I want a job as an accountant, working for a specific accounting firm". She went on to note that she had applied for the position at the accounting firm to no avail. Her dreams were squashed. She had made a conscious decision that she would never fulfil her dream as an accountant based on the negative feedback – no positions available. I could see the disappointment on her face and heard it in her voice as she continued her story. Then I asked, "What do you want most, to become an accountant or to work for the specific accounting firm?" After a moment she responded, "I want to be an accountant". Now we are getting somewhere – pin point her true desire. Since we now "know" her true desire, she was open to applying for an accountant positions at other companies. She now could develop her plan of action and move out to achieve it with confidence.

Some would say, common sense should have told her to apply to other companies. And that is a valid comment, but when your self-confidence is low hearing the word "No" a few times can be stifling. However, when you have clear focus of what you want to achieve it is very easy to be open to other options. Confidence shows up and does not allow you to quit on yourself.

Confidence Trait

Tamar's confidence trait is revealed as we discover that **she knew what she wanted and understood her rights** to the promise.

Time to Reflect and Discuss

Far too many women walk this journey called life never fulfilling their divine calling, their true purpose simply due to the fact that women may often be too indecisive – in other words, double-minded. It is extremely hard to be confident when you don't know what to be confident about – right. Remember, to stand confident is to know that you not only can, but that you will accomplish any task you chose to achieve. Therefore, it is extremely important to take a moment to think about what you want, as well as why you want it. Ask yourself what it will cost you to obtain it; people, resources and time. Is what you want within your rights to have?

Please Read the Biblical Account of Tamar
The Book of Genesis, Chapter 38:1-30
Tamar & Judah

How do I STAND CONFIDENT like Tamar?

1. *What do you want?*

_____

_____

_____

_____

_____

_____

_____

_____

2. *What is the cost to get what you want?*

_____

_____

_____

_____

_____

_____

_____

3. *What are your rights?*

_____

_____

_____

_____

_____

_____

_____

_____

PRAYER

Lord, help me to become a woman of purpose. I look not to my own abilities for you said in your Word that a man's heart plans his way, but the Lord directs his steps (Proverbs 16:9), therefore my desire is that you would reveal to me the steps to take. Show me the purpose you have for my life and allow me to walk worthy of the calling you have placed on my life. I understand it will require me to seek your face by spending time in your Word and in prayer. When you speak to me allow me to hear clearly and to obey your will. In the fear of the Lord there is strong confidence, and His children will have a place of refuge (Proverbs 14:26).

Lord, I know that when you call you equip, therefore let me not become sidetracked or walk in deceitfulness so that your purpose will be fulfilled in my life and those around me. Make your way known to me that I may walk out the journey with confidence.

In Jesus' name I pray,

Amen

3

It's Time To Get Smart About It

RAHAB: The Wise Decision Maker
(Proverbs 3:5-12)

Principle #2 – Wise Decisions Produce Confidence

Have a seat young lady as I begin to share my journey with you. It is a journey unlike any other, for it is mine and mine alone. Yet I am convinced that in between each line you will find a few moments of reminiscence as you see pieces of your story within mine.

It was a shout unlike anything I've heard before. As a peered through the window I watched as the walls of Jericho began to crumble, the noise was like thunder crashing to the ground and the city shook as if an earthquake had hit. I remember hearing the screams of men, women and children outside my door. Safe within the walls of my house my family sat huddled up together, holding on to one another for dear life. I could see the fear in their eyes and on their faces. Tears streamed down the faces of my mother and sisters, yet for some strange reason there was a sense of peace that held me captive; it was a peace which surpasses all understanding.

As if it were yesterday, I recall looking from my window as two handsome men approached the gates, men of whom I had not seen before. They were clothed in robes of royalty, they stood tall and authority was written all over their face. As the two men entered my tavern and took a seat I could see everyone staring wondering from whence they came. I approached their table, "Gentlemen, may I pour you a drink or bring you a bite to eat"? When my eyes meet with the young man seated to my right I could see that there was more here to be discovered, these two were on a mission. It was when I heard his voice that my heart began to race. Israelites.

We knew they would soon arrive. The city of Jericho trembled at the thought of their arrival as we had heard about the mighty deeds of which their God had performed. It is said that the Israelites walked across the river on dry land, yes, the river rose up like a wall, can you believe it, even the waters would not touch the Israelites without permission. Not to mention they utterly destroyed the Kings of Og and Sihon and their kingdom. I needed to know more.

"Gentlemen, will you join me on the rooftop so that I may show you the riches of the land, for you can see all of Jericho from up there". Once up on the rooftop I broke my silence, "So tell me, why have you come to my city, has our hour come?"

My heart sank into my chest and a feeling of anxiety filled my body, a weakness came upon me as they gave me their answer. As they continued to share with me the fate of my city and all its inhabitants, I could hear a disturbance from below. Several city officials had come looking for the men and I knew if they found them there would be no bargaining for my life, so I hid them; deep under the stalks of flax, buried awaiting resurrection. The soldiers called for me, from atop, I came down. With a harsh tone they questioned me concerning the whereabout of the two gentlemen seen entering my tavern. With everything that is within me I tried settling myself before I spoke, I had to be convincing for it would be the death of me and possibly my family should the soldier discover my secret. I lied. At this point, I feared the God of Israel more than the soldiers that stood before me. Maybe, just maybe, if I protected what belongs to the God of Israel, He will protect what belongs to me.

The soldiers were soon on their way, and the gates of Jericho were being shut tight; no one in and no one out. I ran swiftly back to the top of the roof, pulled the stalks of flax from the two spies and began to plead my case.

"The decisions I have made today, if found out will cost me my life, however, I have not only heard about the strength of your God, but also His forgiveness. Therefore, I make this one request, because I have protected you, will you now protect me and my family? A life for a life."

I was told not to share this information with anyone, should I decide to tell of what has happened today, all would come to ruin. It was both a moment of bitterness, yet it was so sweet at the same time. I and my family would live, yet everyone around me, my neighbors, my friends, the children which play at the city gate, the women and men who sell their goods along the streets of Jericho would all be slaughtered.

****

Decisions that Impact

One bad decision could have wiped out the entire city of Jericho, yet because of one woman's confidence in a God she had only heard about, a very small remnant was saved.

Rahab the harlot she is often called, yet an entrepreneur of sorts. She had a few talents; she was an innkeeper, and a crafter of linen (dried stalks of flax were used to make linen cloth).

As I read through her story I thought to myself, this woman sits between a rock and a hard place. She put her life on the line with either decision she made. However, the one smart thing she did that too often women in the decision-making process don't do is Trust God. Because she based her decision on what she understood about the God of Israel, today she is named amongst the great men and women of the bible and became a part of the genealogy of the Messiah, Jesus Christ of Nazareth.

Wise Decisions Produce Confidence

Every day of our lives we are required to make hundreds of decisions. Think about it, from the time you awake until you lay back down to sleep throughout the day you have made decisions which will either affect you in a positive way or will have a negative outcome. I know, you are probably thinking I don't make that many decisions, but let start with just a few...

The alarm clock begins to sound off signaling that it is time for you to get up; will you hit the snooze button, or will you arise? Will you brush your teeth this morning or gurgle with a mouth full of Listerine? Should you take shower or simply get dressed? What outfit will you wear? What pair of shoes will match your outfit? How will you style your hair? Makeup or no makeup? Red or brown lipstick? Will you have a full breakfast or no breakfast at all? Should you take something out for dinner, or will you pick up take out on the way home? Which car will you drive, and which route will you take to your destination today? Wow, so many decisions and you haven't even left the house yet.

Many of our day-to-day decisions are formed out of habit such as those listed above. They are decisions which pose minor or no affect to those around us. However, should you leave the house too many days without brushing or showering you might find that your decision to do so is now impacting others in a major way...lol.

But, what about the decision you are required to make that will greatly impact your life and the lives of others such as your family, a decision like that of Rahab. For example, you are ready to purchase a home. Based on your financial status, your lender has qualified you for up to a $600,000-dollar home. Do you take it, or do you purchase a more reasonably priced home with many of the amenities you'd like but would also allow you to tuck away a few dollars for the future?

Smart decision making does not come easy, its takes practice and as it is said, "practice makes perfect". If you are willing learn from your mistakes as well as the mistakes of others and not let fear of failure stifle you, you will be well on your way to building confidence.

As I took a look back down memory lane of my personal life, I could clearly see the impacts of the decisions I had made; some good, some bad. Those which were good made me proud, I felt like I was on top of my game, yes confident with a capital C. But those which were bad made me want to sweep them under the rug never to be seen again, someone please move them into the land of forgetfulness. One bad decision can be very costly and detrimental to your way of life.

At some point I had to begin to take a close look at the outcome of my decisions. I had to look at my thought process, my emotional state and my spiritual state of mind.

Analyze self? That part right there. It takes a made-up mind, yet a regenerated and an open mind to analyze oneself. Why? Most of us see ourselves as "know it all's". It's true...lol. When we enter into the decision-making process, we enter it alone and we finish it alone - yikes. To many women find themselves making the same mistakes over and over again. Never learning, therefore never building confidence but instead fear is being instilled in their way of thinking.

So how do I make better decisions? I'm glad you asked that question. It begins and end with prayer and listening to the voice of God. I can attest. When I was faced with a decision that would likely impact more than just me, I'd take to prayer. Upon asking the Lord God for His assistance, I was then required to listen and wait for an answer. When I received an answer, I had to stand firm on what I heard and not try to wiggle or squirm my way out of it. If the answer was to move forward, I moved. If I was to stand down, then I did. Yes, it's that simple. Confidence is easy when you are depending on the One that is Higher Than I.

Confidence Trait

Rahab's confident trait is revealed as she ***makes a decision that will impact others based on her reverence of God***.

Time to Reflect and Discuss

The decision-making process requires us to seek wisdom, gain knowledge and apply understanding. All of which are biblically sound decision-making tools. Using Rahab's confidence trait as your example you can almost ensure that your decisions will be sound and precise when your decisions are founded on godly principles. You see, each time you make decisions which results in a positive outcome you will find yourself becoming more confident in the decision-making process.

Please Read the Biblical Account of Rahab
Joshua, Chapter 2:1-21
Rahab and the Spies

How do I STAND CONFIDENT like Rahab?

1. What were your last 3 major decisions?

_____
_____
_____
_____
_____
_____
_____
_____
_____

2. What was the outcome of each of those decisions?

_____
_____
_____
_____
_____
_____
_____
_____
_____

3. Could you have done something better? If so what?

_____
_____
_____
_____
_____
_____
_____
_____
_____

PRAYER

Dear Lord, I come before you as a humble servant, please help me to understand how to make decisions that will impact my life and those around me in a positive way. Allow me to seek your way of doing things as the Word of God says in Matthews 6:33 that I must first seek the Kingdom of God and His righteousness and all these things will be added to me. Give wisdom, knowledge and understanding as I seek you daily in the decision-making process. I know that you Lord are concerned about even the smallest decisions in my life, so continually remind me of your plan for my life so that I may align my decisions to follow suit.

In Jesus' name I pray,

Amen

4

I Am Open To Hear

RUTH: Clear Direction Produces Confidence
(Proverbs 12:15)

Principle #3 – Clear Directions Produce Confidence

Today I consider my mother-in-law to be one of the wises women I have come to know. Wisdom appears like a crown upon her head and confidence covers her feet. It was in a foreign land and amongst a chosen people of whom I barely knew that I would discover the plans for my life, and of what a glorious life I now live.

I lay across my bed filled with sorrow, the love of my youth is no more. Tears flow like a river down my cheeks and I can't seem to stop them. I'm feeling lost, I feel uncovered, I feel unprotected. Who will keep me warm at night when chills of the east winds blow? Who will bring laughter to my morning sparking a song in my heart? Who will fill my belly with life? My love is no more.

Is my life cursed? First my father-in-law, then my brother-in-law and my husband, all dead. What did I do to deserve this kind of life? I was a good wife, I served both the people and the God of my husband to the best of my ability and yet I find myself with no covering, no children and no plans for the future. And now my mother-in-law has requested that I return to my mother's house. I can't go back, I won't go back there is nothing in that place for me.

I watched as my sister-in-law loaded up the donkey and began to walk down the road towards Moab. My heart longed that she would stay as I had come to know her as not simply a sister-in-law but a true friend. I remember turning to my mother-in-law, the compassion that was in her eyes seemed to pierce my soul. She pleaded with me to return as well. I grabbed her around the neck and held her tight, "Naomi, where you go I will go, where you stay I will stay. Your people will be my people and your God will be my God. Where you die, I will die, and there is where we will be buried." God forbid that I would leave this strong and faithful woman alone to suffer all by herself. She has done so much for me, I will repay kindness with kindness; a life for a life.

In the land of which my husband had been born, a place which appears to be prosperous, people were moving all about quickly as though everyone had somewhere of great importance to go. My mother-in-law Naomi and I were greeted by the towns women who were selling their ware. Again, my heart broke as I heard Naomi tell of her plight even to the degree of changing here name; she felt as though the God she served had made her life bitter; a thought which had entered my mind as well.

If we were going to make a life here, I would have to find work, a way to support the both of us. I knew Naomi was far too old for work, so I suggested to her that I find work in the neighboring fields as the barley harvest was beginning. She agreed.

The sun was intense that day, sweat fell from my forehead like streams of flowing water but, a girl must do what a girl must do to survive. This grain field seemed to go on for miles. I was filling my basket very quickly, as I stood up to wipe my brow I could see in the distance an elderly man staring my way. He stood tall and was quite handsome. I assumed he was the owner of the field based on the conversations I overheard from the two women next to me. They mentioned his name, Boaz. I hope he won't make me leave the field, this is the only work I can perform. Oh my, he is coming my way...

I have found favor in the eyes of Boaz, who would have imagined. He has invited me to dinner. The conversation at the table was lively and oh how I enjoyed the company of those gathered around. I had my fill of bread, meat and drink, I still can't believe I'm here. As I began my walk home, I thought to myself, "What a wonderful day it has been, Naomi will be delighted with all I have to tell her".

The journey home was swift; Naomi met me as I opened the door. I told her of the events of the day, but I was not ready for this next move. With detailed directions she told me what I was to do in order to secure my future. Naomi wanted me to be well provided for, so I did exactly what she said, and the results need I say... turned out to be fabulous.

****

Commitment & Direction Leads to Success

There is nothing better than clear and precise direction. Ruth had two major components working on her behalf, (1) she had the voice of reason on her side; her mother-in-law Naomi, and (2) someone close to her that trusted God; yes, and again it was Naomi. Ruth was also committed to the vision that was placed before her and unafraid to walk it out.

Although she was in a land which was unfamiliar Ruth still came out on top. Why? Because she listened and applied what she heard. She could have chosen to do it her way, after all she had been married before; she knew the roles of courtship – so why not do it her way. Ruth was wise enough to know that when in unfamiliar territory it is often best to take advice from someone who knows the land.

I asked myself as I read through Ruth's story, "What caused the young woman to become so committed to Naomi that she would step out on faith, taking direction which would ultimately add her name to the lineage of Jesus Christ?" Well, I believe Ruth, after living with her mother-in-law understood that Naomi was a woman of God. We can see this by Naomi's actions. You see when Naomi heard that God had come to the rescue of her people, she immediately made the decision to make her way back home, back to Bethlehem. During Naomi's life time she had seen God move on the behalf of her people and had come to trust in His provision. She was now teaching Ruth to do the same.

Commitment Exudes Confidence

Commitment has a partner whose name is direction. The confident woman is notorious for attempting to go it alone. She knows what she wants, has made the decision to go after her dreams and is committed, but this one thing I have learned from experience, so I pass this tidbit along to you... "Get clear direction." What's your plan girlfriend?

Without clear direction you are sure to get "lost in the sauce." Take a moment to plan it out what that dream really looks like. Nobody ever starts a trip without first looking at their map (I'm telling my age again...lol), ok without typing the address into their GPS. Just as your GPS maps out turn for turn, so should your goal be planned, well that's if you want to complete it. A true plan details the start, the process in between and tells you when you should complete. Notice, your GPS tells you at what time you are expected to arrive and will even let you know if there is an accident up ahead, which may require you to reroute. Clear direction does the exact same thing.

Now, one other question to consider, before we leave this discussion... Who is directing you? I know, I know, if you are anything like me, "You've got this." But what I discovered was that I didn't have it, primarily because I did not have an accountability partner or a mentor to run my thoughts pass; someone who knew more than I. Therefore, I kept operating in a dysfunctional manner.

My friend let me tell you, having an accountability partner or mentor... it's called operating with wisdom. I am not suggesting that you let someone do all the thinking for you and that you should not have a say in how your goals get accomplished, but I have found it to be a great help when I can run ideas pass my mentor and allow someone to critique my work. Someone who will tell you the truth. It is okay to ask for help.

I am taken back to my early twenties, which now seem so long ago, but I remember this conversation as though it were yesterday. I had recently divorced after two years of marriage (yikes – young and in love but with no direction) and two children later. My eldest sister Leola and I were standing in the driveway of my parent's house discussing matters of life when she said to me, "Lisa, don't ever wait for anyone to give you what you want, work for it and go get it". Words of wisdom from a wise woman, and words that I have lived by – little did I know she was teaching me a biblical principle. Her words were not just a statement, as she was a living example of what she had spoken which allowed me to see the road ahead of me just a little clearer – simply one of my Ruth and Naomi moments, I've had many – Praise God.

Confidence Trait

Ruth's confidence trait is revealed as we discover that **she was committed and adhered to the direction** of Naomi.

Time to Reflect and Discuss

Confidence arises when we become committed to the task at hand. You may think that knowing what you want and making a decision to go after your dreams is enough to thrust you forward, but truth be told simply making a decision is hardly enough.

We as women make decisions constantly, yet we often lack the follow through. This is because the decisions of the mind can often be fleeting thoughts. When you become serious about your vision, you must also commit to the vision. I have found that on a personal level, when I commit to completing a goal, the resources begin to show up. When you are committed you tend to be willing to go the extra mile, and the statement, "By whatever means necessary" become your mantra. Your "will becomes the way" and if that doesn't work you are willing to try something else until you get the job done. At this point of commitment, you are confident that you will succeed, and no one will be able to tell you otherwise.

Please Read the Biblical Accounts of Ruth
Ruth, Chapter 3:1-18
Ruth and Boaz at the Threshing Floor

How do I STAND CONFIDENT like Ruth?

1. **List 3 tasks that you have committed to achieve?**

_____
_____
_____
_____
_____
_____
_____
_____

2. **Do you have clear direction to complete those tasks?**

_____
_____
_____
_____
_____
_____
_____

3. **Who is holding you accountable? Are they a reliable source?**

_____
_____
_____
_____
_____
_____
_____
_____

PRAYER

Dear Lord, I thank you for providing clear direction for my life. For allowing me to hear the voice of the Holy Spirit clearly and to walk in a spirit of obedience. Your Word tells me in Proverbs 3:6 to acknowledge you in all my ways and You Lord will direct my path. I pray that you will send godly men and women into my life who will lead by example, through wisdom, knowledge and understanding that will first direct me to you and then towards achieving my personal goals.

Show me how I can become more committed to completing the goals and tasks which are set before me and to help others do the same. Let me not be anxious for anything, but to come before you in prayer concerning every detail of my life (Philippians 4:6) that I may walk in confidence.

In the name of Jesus, I Pray,

Amen

5

I Can Follow Your Lead

BATHSHEBA: The Company You Keep
(Proverbs 24:6)

Principle #4 – Surround Yourself With People Of Influence

This wasn't the way I thought my life would turn out. I've been through quite an ordeal over the past few years. Never in my wildest dream would I have thought I'd sit on the throne next to a King as his wife. My journey to the throne was by no means a normal account; lust, fear, death, a heavy heart, love and more death – can you say, "Wow". To tell you my entire story would take some time to do, so I will share with you how I discovered peace and moved swiftly with confidence.

My heart almost stopped as he told me the news; the birth rights of my son, swept away. Upon the throne sits another man, his brother Adonijah to be exact. If Adonijah becomes king, he is sure to take the life of my son as well as my life. This predicament is more than my heart can withstand. However, the decision is not final until my husband decrees it so.

As I sat in my boudoir pondering, I thought, "should I take the advice of the Nathan the priest and go before the king concerning this matter? Everyone knows that I must be summoned by the king, I can't simply show up." But if I do nothing, I am sure to regret my decision. Let me prepare... I'm going to see the king whether called for or not as the results could ultimately be the same – death. I will take that chance.

As I walked toward the Kings chamber, I went over again and again in mind what Nathan the priest had me to rehearse. You see Nathan, a priest to the king was highly educated and noted for his wisdom. He and the other priest sat amongst each other and frequently address the issues of the kingdom. The King respected him and often took his advice verbatim, so with that in mind, I will do the same.

I remember shaking so bad and I felt faint as I entered the King's chamber. I just knew this would be the end of me, I dare not look up. I kept my head low and I bowed even lower, waiting for the king to speak, and he did. *"What is it you want?"*, he asked. I let out a sigh of relief and begin to tell him of my plight just as Nathan had advised. But before I could finish Nathan rushed into the room and began to share the same information, he told the story with much more zeal than I and with such persistence that the king stood up and made a decree of expedience.

To my delight, this issue was resolved quickly and to my favor. I stand in the courtroom, a proud mother as my son Solomon is made king. I will forever be indebted to Nathan the priest for his wisdom and guidance concerning the matter at hand.

****

Through Mentorship We Learn To Stand Confident

It is not always easy to think straight in times of distress. Queen Bathsheba found herself in a predicament which was not self-induced, yet it was another life or death situation for her. She could have decided to take matters into her own hands and act out of an emotional state as far too many women do and thereby causing much different results.

Bathsheba knew she was in the company of wisemen. I'm sure the palace was full of them as her husband King David surrounded himself with men of valor, wisdom and stature. Men he could depend on to do and say the right thing at the right time. Yes, men of integrity. On many occasions she probably witnessed Nathan in action and had seen the outcome of his decisions and insight, therefore she knew that Nathan had a way with the king. Therefore, she would use King David and Nathan's bond to her advantage.

Knowledge Builds Confidence

When you know better, you do better. I once read, "The sum of who you are can clearly be seen by the people of which you surround yourself". You begin to look like them, you talk like them, you dress like them and your attitude and character are driven by them. So, I ask you, who's your them? Consider the five closest people in your circle, are they adding value to your life or simply sucking the life out of you. Are they helping you in any way to achieve your goals or life purpose? If your answer to those last two question airs on the positive side, you've been blessed, but if on the negative, it's time for change, its time to do better.

I know from experience change isn't always easy and attempting to change your social circle is even more challenging because you might not know where to start. It's going to take you stepping out in confidence and believing that you deserve the best out of life so that you can give the best from your life. If you don't grow, if you don't develop how can you expect to grow, develop and lead others – the golden rule in action. Let's look at a few suggestions on how to get started.

Mentorship. Mentors and coaches are everywhere – and that is good for us! Yes, I have a mentor, make that mentors. When I took a look at my social and personal circle (can be one in the same) I discovered that the people around me could not help me as they were far too busy trying to help themselves, personally, financially and spiritually. I knew I had to, "Level Up". I began to seek out a mentor, someone who was well versed, advanced and already doing or had done what I was attempting to pursue as a career. I did my research, prayed about it and asked God to reveal to me where and which person would be most beneficial for my growth. With the direction of the Lord I found more than one mentor; a few of which I had to pay dearly for their service and others which imparted knowledge and wisdom freely that if I had paid for would have cost me a fortune.

Your mentor should cause you to have continuous vision shifts. They should challenge you and dare you to think and rethink your purpose and goals. They should stress that in many cases you must walk the corridor alone to achieve the greatest growth, knowing that the voice of wisdom and reason is waiting outside the door, and will rush in to command attention when necessary...

Mastermind Groups or Meet-ups. I cannot stress how important it is to surround yourself with forward thinking people to build your confidence. Mastermind groups or Meet- up groups are designed to help you think out-loud and provide a voice of reason should you find yourself stagnated or moving in the wrong direction. A good group will normally consist of a leader or several leaders that keep the group organized, on topic and moving forward with purpose.

Stay clear of negative Nancy groups – you are seeking to grow.

Higher Education. Education by way of simply definition… "to seek out the truth". Truths enhance every area of our lives; personal, spiritual, and financially. Just because you graduated high school doesn't mean you stop developing your mind. There is still more learning to be done even after you complete college no matter the level. Educating one's self is a lifelong process. I know you may be saying to yourself, I don't have that kind of money… I say to you, "How bad do you want IT." Whatever that IT might be. It's time to do some research, there are scholarships, grants, employee benefits from your employer just to name a few. Start with a community college, but whatever you do get started. It's not about the degree… it's about the knowledge you gain. Some of you may not want full blown college degrees and to be truthful you may not need one, but you can always develop the skills that you have – so take a course or two.

I speak to you from experience, as I mentioned I have several mentors, I host as well as participate in mastermind and meet-up groups, and I am continuously taking courses to develop my skills. It helped my confidence soar even higher – I'm just saying.

Confidence Trait

Bathsheba's confidence trait is revealed as we discover that **she took wise counsel**.

Time to Reflect and Discuss

The last time you found yourself in a sticky situation did you fold, or did you grow? I recall an incident when my daughter had been notified by the school that my grandson could not be found on the school grounds. Imagine the panic; it was just that sheer panic. My daughter called me with terror in her voice and as I calmed her down just enough to hear what she was saying, terror ran through me as well. I dropped to my knees and cried out, "No". It was almost simultaneously that as I yelled out and dropped to my knees that I also got my bearings back. I stood up very quickly as I heard that inner voice tell me to get more information before I allowed panic to seize my emotion and cause me to make irrational decisions. You see I had been in the presence of many great leaders; my mentor, my spiritual and workplace leadership, as well as several educators all of whom had taught me to think through the process before making a final decision. The people you surround yourself with will either bring life or death to your situations. Whatever you surround yourself with is what you will become. As the old adage goes, "Birds of a feather flock together", and I will add... they all end up in the same place.

The Biblical Account of Bathsheba
1 Kings, Chapter 1:11-31
David & Bathsheba

How do I STAND CONFIDENT like Bathsheba?

1.   To complete your goals are you required to gain more insight or knowledge? How will you obtain more knowledge?

_____

_____

_____

_____

_____

_____

_____

2.   Even Mentors need coaching. Who is your Mentor?

_____

_____

_____

_____

_____

_____

_____

3.   Does your Mentor inspire you to change? In what way?

_____

_____

_____

_____

_____

_____

_____

PRAYER

In your presence Lord there is fullness of joy. May you grant me the opportunity to live a life that is pleasing towards you. As I begin to seek out wisdom, I am reminded that wisdom begins first of all with the fear of God (Psalm 111:10). Allow knowledgeable people to enter into my surrounding, people of whom have a desire to grow and develop me, those who would assist me in fulfilling the purpose in which you have for my life. Bring strong men and women across my path which will cultivate and build me into a more confident woman.

My desire is to increase my learning, to become an educated woman therefore in doing so, I need your direction Lord to guide me to the proper learning institution or programs as well as provide the resources for my expenses. Let me not squander any resource that you place into my hands, but let it be used for the building of the Kingdom of God and to the Glory of God.

In Jesus' name I pray,

Amen

6

I Believe It

Mary: The Vision Birthed
(Hebrews 11:1)

Principle #5 – Confidence Without Faith Is Dead

It was an ordinary day, yet an extraordinary moment in my life. Never in my wildest dreams would I have considered that I would be chosen for such a work, for such a miraculous and life-changing experience to conceive and birth a child which would have the ability to produce change in everyone. May I share?

A girl could not have been happier than I. Joseph, who was not only tall, dark and handsome but was a man who knew the voice of God had selected me to be his bride. Every day I woke with excitement as my mother and I planned out the wedding. I would adorn myself with fine silk and linens from the neighboring women who sold at the city gate – scarlet red, blues and majestic purples with a trace of gold on the trim. Yes, it would be the ceremony of all ceremonies!

As I stood in my room preparing to go with my mother to the market I was startled as he appeared. No not Joseph... but an Angel. He was breathe taking and a wonder to behold, I wondered what I could have done to have caused such a visitation from a heavenly host. I was both captivated, speechless and even a little afraid when he the Angel Gabriel began to tell me the purpose of his visit.

I can't explain it but within the same measure of time came confession and clarity. It was at that moment that I discovered a since of purpose. I had found favor with the God of all creation; I wanted what He wanted, I decided at that moment to align myself with the words and vision that was placed before me, that I would listen to instructions and abide, that I would say, "Yes" to birthing the savior of this world.

As quickly as he appeared, he, the Angel Gabriel disappeared.

I pinched myself, did that really happen or am I dreaming. Me, little ole Mary, to become the mother of the Lord whose kingdom will never end. How will I ever explain this to Joseph? Who is going to believe such a story? Never the less, it will be so.

"Jesus" what a stately name.

****

In Christ all things are possible

Mary understood three major components of living a confident lifestyle, 1). She believed the vision was from God, 2). She believed the vision was for her to fulfill, and 3). She believed that the manifestation of the vision would impact everyone who was exposed to it. Take note of the common phase, "she believed".

What I love must about Mary's story is that she didn't wait on the opinion of others to guide her; she received her instructions from God and allowed His word to be final instructions for her life. Her belief system allowed her to step out in faith – she trusted the process and the process produced results. She took ownership of the vision, she excepted that she was worthy enough (she found favor with God), that she could be used by God to get the task at hand accomplished. She did not, and I repeat did not begin to take inventory on her personal abilities nor did she compare herself to anyone as she knew that God had qualified her and that was more than enough. If God said it... that settles it!

Nor did she run and tell everyone – listen ladies, listen.

Faith, When Self-Confidence Meets Godliness

Mary said "Yes" to the vision! Why because she was first confident in the vision giver. You see self-confidence is good, yet it will only take you as far as your ability allows but coupling self-confidence with your faith (I can do all things through Christ Jesus who strengthens me – Phil 4:13) will cause you to move mountains.

Mary received, conceived, nurtured and birthed the vision – let us use the process of childbirth as a metaphor as to how a vision is birthed.

- Conception: the seed or thought is planted
- Cultivation: the vision develops and begins to take shape.
- Labor: facing opposition trying to hold back the vision – push girl!
- Birth: delivering a breathing, living entity – life.

This is the simplified process, for those of you which have already had children know there is so much more to the birthing process and that everyone woman's birthing experience is her own – similar yet oh so different. Having said that, you must come to the realization that most dreams don't come true overnight, they take time. Know this, it is okay to take your time as you don't want to miss the mark. Moving with haste may cause you to miscarriage – and nobody wants that.

Confidence Built By Faith

Faith is literally the substance of which your confidence is built on. To get anything of relevance accomplished in life you will need to operate through the eyes of faith – right. Think about it, in order to accomplish anything, you must first *believe* it can be done. Confidence by Webster's definition: a). a feeling or consciousness of one's powers or of reliance on one's circumstances, b). faith or belief that one will act in a right, proper, or effective way, and c). the quality or state of being certain

Confidence produced through faith is extremely powerful because its only fuel is vision. Vision produces strength, character, clarity, creativity, resourcefulness, joy, harmony and so much more. Yes, that image, that goal which at one time seemed impossible now becomes "the possible".

As you step out to complete any vision, dream or goal, you will be faced with many hurdles and obstacles in which you must overcome such as insecurity, fear, resource availability, and rejection just to name a few. Now, you could continue to focus on the negative of which everyone knows that negative thinking will keep you stuck, but let us focus on the positive like Mary did.

In 2002, I sat at the top of the staircase in my home wondering how I was going to provide for my children Nela and Nina. I had stretched my budget as far as it could go, yet my weekly paycheck never seemed to be enough to cover all the expenses. I remember sitting there on that staircase asking God how I could make ends meet. I did not want to take on another job outside of the home because I could not bear to leave my children alone yet another six to eight hours more per day. I was just about to give up hope when I heard these words, "PJs in a sack". I kid you not... as if someone was standing beside me whispering in my ear. There the voice was again repeating, "PJs in a sack". So I repeated out loud what I'd heard, but with question, "What is PJs in a sack"? Ladies, can I tell you... clarity came quick. I jumped up, ran to my sewing room and created a "PJ In A Sack" (matching pajamas top and bottom with a back-sack), and the rest was history. I started my first home-based business, which was fueled by continual divine vision and purpose. I got out of debt quickly, and began my new found journey of learning and understanding financial responsibility and business development. Low-and-behold that one simple vision point evolved and assisted in leading me to become the confident business woman I am today, teaching other women to be bold, courageous, fabulous and to walk with confidence.

That particular vision went from zero to one-hundred quickly, but not all of my experiences have been the same, some took a few months others a few years to evolve.

On the stairs, I did four specific things, 1). I asked God (our highest authority) for clarity, 2). I received an answer, a vision, 3). I moved out on the vision, I said "Yes", and 4). advanced to a place where others are now benefiting from the vision.

The confidence produced through a faith-based lifestyle will cause you to confront situations and circumstances with a different mindset. Why, because you know it's not just about you, but it is about the vision and the accomplishment of the vision which will impact the lives of others in a positive way. Your mindset shifts from me – to we.

Be Confident In Who You Are

Confidence produced through faith will also cause you to understand who you are. You are designed with vision and a purpose that only you can fulfil. There is no one like you! Even if you have a twin or a sibling in which you resemble there are major differences in your character and personality – so I repeat there is no one like you. Stop comparing yourself to other people. You don't need to have what they have, or look like they look, or do what they do. Discover what God has planned for you and give it your all. I know you are bombarded with social media and television always telling you that lifestyles other than your own are more glamorous and fulfilling, don't give in to the lies and distractions. So I say to you today – "YOU ARE MORE THAN ENOUGH JUST THE WAY YOU ARE."

But, I guess the real take away from this chapter is… "True confidence can only be found in knowing Christ Jesus as Lord and Savior of your life. To know Him is to eventually discover who you are."

Confidence Trait

Mary's confidence trait is revealed as we discover that **she took ownership and dared to believe**.

Time to Reflect and Discuss

Now faith is confidence in what we hope for and assurance about what we do not see. (Hebrews 11:1)". You must first understand that it takes faith to step out on any vision or dream, yes, it takes true confidence. And because faith is an action word it requires you to not only focus on the vision but begin to move towards a vision which has been seen only as a mental picture. Who does that... A Confident Woman.

Please Read
The Biblical Account of Mary the Mother of Jesus
Luke, Chapter 1:26-38
Mary and the Angel Gabriel

How do I STAND CONFIDENT like Mary?

1. Do you believe you can achieve your goals? Why?

_____
_____
_____
_____
_____
_____
_____
_____
_____

2. Do you believe you hear the voice of God speaking? Give an example.

_____
_____
_____
_____
_____
_____
_____
_____
_____

3. When was the last time you stepped out in faith to achieve a goal? What were the results?

_____
_____
_____
_____
_____
_____
_____
_____
_____

PRAYER

NOW FAITH is the substance of things hoped for, the evidence of things not seen (Hebrews 11:1). Dear Lord, I stand before you with a humbled heart, with an understanding that you Lord know the plans you have for me, plans which are for my good and not for harm (Jerimiah 29:11). As I put my trust in you, seek your face and ask for the leading of the Holy Spirit, I can step out in faith believing that the desires of my heart are untainted before you. I believe you chose me and have called me to fulfill the purpose that you have for my life. Because you have called me Lord, my answer to your call is YES.

In Jesus' name I pray,

Amen

7

Her Unique Confidence

The Balcony Experience
(Romans 12:1-21)

Confidence - The dream process begins with a simple thought, which then leads to pondering of the possibilities of what the future might hold. It is that glimpse of the dream that thrust us forward and to walk confidently after our pursuit.

You may have discovered by now that this book actually has very little to do with high heels and everything to do with becoming confident through the leading of the scripture given to us by the one and true Living God.

Confidence is a state of being. It is that character trait that moves you from standing still to living out loud.

Each woman in the previous chapters, Tamar, Rahab, Ruth, Bathsheba and Mary each had their very own story to tell, and they each offered up their very own unique confidence style in the effort to take hold of their dream. The first four women made up in their mind to go after the desire of their heart, and eventually obtained what they were pursuing, but not without a struggle. Mary on the other hand was commissioned. She listened closely to the instructions that were given to her by the Lord God. She accepted what was spoken and therefore the promise given to her was fulfilled – no pressure. I share this nugget with you because I want to remind you that there is no greater confidence boost than the boost you will receive when you are obedient to the voice of

God. When you come to the place where you stop telling God what you want and begin to ask Him what He wants from your life, it is at that point that you move from simply being "Confident" to being "Godfident".

You too have your own unique confidence journey. The story of your life which can only be experienced and told by you. Some women are extremely confident, while others are still battling with fear, yet it does not matter which level of confidence you possess, you can always improve. Applying the five building blocks contained in the chapters of this book will cause you to step out on faith and begin to pursue your dreams with the understanding that your dreams are obtainable.

As I stated in the opening of the book, you were design on purpose, with purpose to fulfill a purpose. A purpose which can only be fulfilled by you. I want you to take a moment to really think about that statement. The Lord God in all of His wisdom, created you to be undeniably unique. He put His signature on you, noting that you are "good". Go back and read chapters one through two of the Book of Genesis in the Bible so that you can be reminded that everything God created is good which includes you. Everything about you is so unique that there is only one you – its kind of funny and I often laugh out loud about it, because in all honesty there is no comparison to you. I will say it again... even if you are a twin, she may look like you, but she is not you. Therefore, you can stop comparing yourself to others. Stop using someone else's measuring rod to measure your accomplishments, your beauty, your business, your education or anything else for that matter. Stand confident in who you are.

I believe the Lord God gave me this message to share, this message of encouragement and empowerment, this message of confidence because I've experienced firsthand too many women comparing themselves to me, even to the point of downplaying their abilities and who they have been designed to be. I am tired of it ladies, so I am here to tell you, you are not supposed to be like me, look like me, dress like me, smell like me, talk or walk like me – you are designed to be the "Fabulous You". Now of course there are attributes and characteristics of my life or the life of others you might admire, but you must come to the realization of how special and beautiful you are, and let no one, and I mean no one take that away from you – Stand Confident.

Now, as you wrap yourself in confidence be sure not to become overzealous in confidence that you begin to think of yourself more highly than you should. Consider this, every person carries the same measure of value – that value given to them by the Lord God. It is not your duty to judge or compare their journey to yours as each person's journey is designed to be different. Every person of whom God has created is necessary and I've come to the conclusion that it is better to build a person up rather than tear them down.

Confident woman, if you will purpose in your heart to focus on the plans which God has for you, it will leave very little time for you to focus on the plans the Lord God has for everyone else. I guarantee you that in staying focused on your purpose, it will take a great load of worry off your shoulders. Start by discovering who you really are, not by who everyone else says you should be. Start by asking yourself the question, "What do I want", then go after your dreams and don't let anyone get in the way. Remember the four steps that follow knowing what you want; become a good decision maker, get direction, get educated, and last but not least... birth the dream.

As I sat on the balcony of the hotel a new chapter in the journey of my life was introduced to me. Little did I know that within less than two short years of "the balcony experience" women from across the United States would be contacting me requesting mentorship with a desire to understand how they could walk more confidently in the call on their life. I began to share this book years before it was completed; in conferences, in small gatherings as well as from behind the pulpit, and having done so, I truly hope the message in this book has been a blessing and inspiration to the both the hearer and reader.

I knew that out on that balcony the Lord God had equipped me with the tools for confident living and that my purpose in life was to share the message He had given me. It was at that moment, with that knowing, I made the decision to follow after the leading of the Holy Spirit versus trying to get the Lord God to bless and go along with my personal plans, you know... the things in life I wanted to do. With purpose and determination, I chose to submit to the Will of God, it was the best decision I've made yet, and boy what a confidence boost. It was on the balcony that I discovered I wore Heels Too High on purpose.

Heels Too High

A Love Note to The Reader from Alesia

The most confident women in the world are those who rest in Christ Jesus. In my early teens I was introduced to Christ. It was a moment that changed my life forever, to the degree that I am still walking out the measure of faith that was given to me. New-birth in Christ Jesus.

This one moment impacted my life in such a way that I want to share the love of God with you. I pray that you already know the Lord Jesus Christ as you Lord and Savior, but if you don't and you would like to... read on!

Live An Abundant Life In Jesus

4 Things God Wants You To Know

1) You Need to Be Saved! "All have sinned and come short of the glory of God" (Romans 3:23). "There is not a just man upon earth, that does good, and sins not" (Ecclesiastes 7:20). "Except a man be born again, he cannot see the kingdom of God" (John 3:3).

2) You Cannot Save Yourself! "Not by works of righteousness which we have done, but according to His mercy He saved us" (Titus 3:5). "By the works of the law shall no flesh be justified" (Galatians 2:16). "Jesus saith unto him, I am the way, the truth, and the life: no man cometh unto the Father, but by Me" (John 14:6).

3) Jesus Can Save You! "Christ . . . hath once suffered for sins, the just for the unjust, that He might bring us to God" (1 Peter 3:18). "God so loved the world, that He gave His only begotten Son, that whosoever believeth in Him should not perish, but have everlasting life" (John 3:16).

4) Trust Jesus Now! "Seek ye the Lord while He may be found, call ye upon Him while He is near" (Isaiah 55:6). "Behold, now is the day of salvation" (2 Corinthians 6:2). "What shall it profit a man, if he shall gain the whole world, and lose his own soul?" (Mark 8:36). Repent (accept God's view of your need): "Except ye repent, ye shall all likewise perish" (Luke 13:3).

Believe: "Believe on the Lord Jesus Christ, and thou shalt be saved, and thy house" (Acts 16:31).

Confess Jesus as Your Lord: "If thou shalt confess with thy mouth the Lord Jesus, and shalt believe in thine heart that God hath raised Him from the dead, thou shalt be saved" (Romans 10:9).

Remember: "Every one of us shall give account of himself to God" (Romans 14:12). "It is appointed unto men once to die, but after this the judgment" (Hebrews 9:27).

"Choose you this day whom ye will serve" (Joshua 24:15)

About the Author

Alesia Dowden, "The Confidence Coach" is a Woman of God, a Wife, Mother, Grandmother, Mentor and Author. She is the founder and owner of Alesia Dowden Enterprise [ADE]. ADE is an organization which is dedicated to assisting women from all walks of life in personal and leadership development. Alesia believes that everyone woman is born with purpose and has a purpose which must be fulfilled in order to live the best life possible; one that will continually add value to others.

Her personal goal is to help others discover their purpose and passion by providing several forms of informative exposure. Alesia offers workshops, seminars, and coaching, to assist in aiding personal and professional growth through study and practical application of proven leadership methods.

Alesia has held several key roles within one of the Fortune 500 Aerospace Companies and has offered senior management alternative solutions to their cost issues as well as overseeing special projects. Her expertise..."Turning matters of chaos into streamlined processes".

In 2002, Alesia began her first entrepreneurial venture. She merged my analytical and business skills with her creative crafting skills and started her first home-based business, "Stitches". It was a success, but she knew she had more to offer. Alesia discovered that she had a strong desire to help develop people. Since that time, she has been on a mission to help women that are pursuing their dreams by assisting them in realizing their hidden potential.

Alesia holds a bachelor's degree in Business Management and a master's degree in Business Administration both from the University of Phoenix. She is also a trained and certified John Maxwell Team Speaker, Trainer and Coach. She holds the position of Board of Director for two (2) non-profit organizations in Los Angeles County.

Her Purpose:
To provide leadership, information and resources by which any woman can enhance her lifestyle.

Her Core Values:
*Integrity is key in all relationships
*Direct, open and honest communication
*Every great leader must be a great servant
*Empower others to lead
*Self and Spiritual Awareness

Discover More About Alesia Dowden

www.ALESIADOWDEN.com

Other Books by Alesia Dowden

Entrepreneur Extraordinaire. This incredible resource will support your success, enhance your productivity and effectiveness and give you tools for communicating and cultivating customer relationships and strategic alliances. Regardless of where you are in your business, you will surely benefit from the information in this book.

This book can be purchased online at www.alesiadowden.com/shop

<hr/>

KEEP WATCH FOR ALESIA'S NEXT BOOK!

58910098R00046

Made in the USA
Columbia, SC
27 May 2019